DESIGNS FOR

BEADED JEWELLERY

USING NATURAL MATERIALS

DESIGNS FOR

BEADED JEWELLERY

USING NATURAL MATERIALS

MARIA DI SPIRITO

SEARCH PRESS

First published in Great Britain 2006 by Search Press Limited,
Wellwood, North Farm Road, Tunbridge Wells, Kent TN2 3DR

Originally published in Italy 2005 by Il Castello Collane Tecniche, Milan

English translation by Karen Waloschek in association with
First Edition Translations Ltd, Cambridge

ISBN-10: 1-84448-163-8
ISBN-13: 978-1-84448-163-7

Photography by G. Cigolini

All the jewellery in this book was made from materials supplied by
FANTASY CRAFT of Milan, www.fantasycraft.it

Printed by Leo Paper Products Ltd, China

Contents

Introduction

In this beautiful book, Maria di Spirito presents an exquisite collection of beaded jewellery designs, all created using natural materials such as semi-precious stones, coral, madrepore, wood, mother-of-pearl and string combined with contemporary yarns and components. With forty-eight original designs for necklaces, bracelets, rings and earrings to choose from, in a spectrum of styles that includes luminous, colourful, extravagant, ethnic, classical, elegant, romantic and sporty, jewellery lovers will be unable to resist the temptation to create something for themselves, or as a gift for someone special.

The aim of this book is not to be a technical manual, but more to provide the experienced jewellery maker with a range of new ideas and ways of combining materials and colours in their own designs. Those who are new to jewellery making, on the other hand, will find within its pages all the inspiration they need to try out this exciting and rewarding craft for themselves.

Whether you choose to reproduce each item exactly as it is shown in the picture, or would prefer to use just some of the ideas featured, all you need to do is look carefully at the full-page picture, and take note of the details shown in the smaller photographs. After that, simply allow your imagination to flow, allowing yourself to be guided by the various shapes, colours and materials used to create your own, personal collection of beaded jewellery.

Maria di Spirito

Black necklaces with mother-of-pearl pendants

Twist a braid from 5 threads of glass and wooden beads. Pass the threads through the mother-of-pearl pendant so they come out at the bottom. Finish the threads with little speckled seashells.

Designer: Maria di Spirito

Difficulty level: medium

Materials:

0.35mm nylon thread
Glass and wooden beads
Glass seed beads
Glass bugle beads
Mother-of-pearl pendants
Spring clasp with chain
Speckled seashells

Tools:

Flat nose pliers
Scissors

Designer beads with mother-of-pearl pendant

Thread beads on to lengths of string and make 8 groupings of assorted beads using knots to space them apart. Halfway through, add a mother-of-pearl pendant. Finish with a buttonhole fastening.

Difficulty level: easy

Designer: Claudia Galanti

Materials:

0.8mm and 10mm string
Transparent gold and 4mm black crystals
Large decorated beads
Round glass and avventurine beads
Resin seashell pendant

Tools:

Scissors

Wooden bead necklace with mother-of-pearl pendant

Make up 4 threads of alternating wooden beads, seed beads and mother-of-pearl buttons. Join the 4 threads together in a large wooden bead and pass through the pendant's hole to make a ring of seed beads. Close the ends with a spring clasp.

Difficulty level: medium

Designer: Maria di Spirito

Materials:

0.35mm nylon thread
Ivory iridescent seed beads
Mother-of-pearl buttons and pendant
Variously shaped and coloured wooden beads
Clamshell bead tips and spring clasp

Tools:

Scissors
Flat nose pliers

Luanus shells and iridescent seed beads

For the pink necklace make up 10 nylon threads with glass beads and pink shells. Feed the 10 threads into a pendant and finish with 5 threads. Fasten the strands with spiral bead tips and a spring clasp.

Difficulty level: medium   Designer: Maria di Spirito

Luanus shell necklace designed by: Paola Feletti

Materials for pink necklace:

0.25mm nylon thread
Pale topaz shimmering seed beads
Pink seashells, pink seashell mosaic pendant
Spiral bead tips, spring clasps and chain

Materials for the curly shell necklace:

0.8mm twisted, waxed cotton thread
8mm amber glass beads
1 string of luanus shells

Tools:

Flat nose pliers
Scissors

Popcorn luanus shell and mother-of pearl necklace

Make up 12 threads of popcorn luanus shells and group the shells together separated by knots and mother-of-pearl discs. Add a mother-of-pearl pendant. Finish the threads with the bead tips and a hook and eye clasp. For the bracelet, thread the shells on two rounds of memory wire.

Difficulty level: easy

Designer: Valeria Castelli

Materials:

0.8mm white 'Fantasy' yarn
1 string of popcorn luanus shells
Mother-of pearl discs and pendant
Bead tips
Hook and eye clasp
Memory wire

Tools:

Flat nose pliers
Scissors

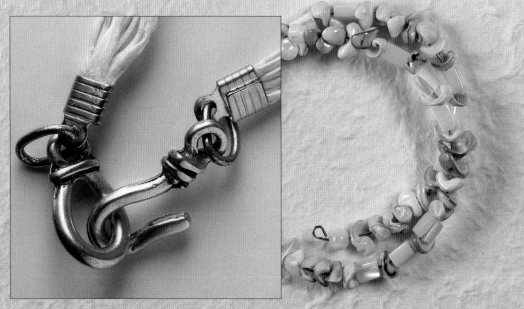

17

Sky blue seashell necklaces

For the necklace with the blue stone pendant, make up 4 groups of shells and space them apart by alternating knots and blue howlite stones. Then attach the pendant to the middle. Finish with a hook and eye catch.

Difficulty level: easy

Designer: Valeria Castelli

For the necklace with the stone and shell cluster, thread shell and blue howlite stone fragments on to metal wire and place the cluster at the centre.

Difficulty level: medium

Designer: Licia Fontana

Materials for the necklace with centrepiece:

0.8mm white 'Fantasy' yarn
A string of blue dyed seashell fragments
Blue howlite stones and pendant ring
Bead tips
Hook and eye clasp

Materials for the flower necklace:

0.8mm gold coloured metal wire
0.8mm 'Fantasy' yarn in blue and in white
A string of blue dyed seashell fragments
A string of blue howlite stones
Little shell cups
Spring clasp and chain

Tools:

Wire cutters
Flat nose pliers
Scissors

Cornelian shells pendant

Use a round metal filigree disc as the base for the shells and cornelian chips centrepiece. Hang from 2 threads of rattail and 2 threads of twine decorated with knots and groups of cornelian and avventurine stones.

Difficulty level: medium

Designer: Neria Lumiati

Materials:

Brown rattail
Orange twine
0.5mm wire
1 thread cornelian chips
1 thread avventurine chips
1 thread of shells
Small clamshell bead tips
Metal filigree disc
Pins and little rings
Spring clasp

Tools:

Wire cutters
Flat nose pliers
Round nose pliers
Scissors

Sky blue and mother-of-pearl

Make up 7 threads with drum-shaped wooden beads, little shells and blue seed beads. Attach 3 rings made up of beads to the pendant and pass the made up threads through these rings to make the necklace. Finish with wooden beads, a spring clasp and chain.

Difficulty level: easy

Designer: Maria di Spirito

Materials:

0.3mm nylon thread
Blue drum-shaped wooden beads
Blue wooden beads
1 thread each of shell chips and small shells
Seed beads in 2 shades of blue
Mother-of-pearl pendant
Spring clasp and chain

Tools:

Flat nose pliers
Scissors

23

Mother-of-pearl and dichromatic glass

Twist some metal wire around the large dichromatic glass bead. Make a ring on the rear face of the stone through which to pass the necklace. Prepare a string, and knot crystals into it at regular intervals. If desired, add some coloured 'Fantasy' yarns and knot together with the crystal-strung string at regular intervals. Add some round mother-of-pearl discs and finish with bead tips and a spring clasp.

Difficulty level: medium   Designer: Amarilli Reggiani

Materials:

Metal wire
1mm string
6mm rose-cut half crystal

'Fantasy' yarns
Mother-of-pearl discs
Dichromatic glass pendant
Bead tips and spring clasps

Tools:

Flat nose pliers
Scissors

Pearls, shells and seeds

For the white necklace, alternate groups of imitation pearls, seeds and glass beads, and separate the groups with knots. Finish with a buttonhole fastener.

Difficulty level: easy

Designer: Valeria Castelli

For the necklace with the shell pendant, make up a helicoidal tube with seed beads and bugle beads on brandy coloured steel wire.

Difficulty level: complex

Designer: Daniela Costa

Materials for the white necklace:

0.8mm brown 'Fantasy' yarn
1 string tropical seeds
0.8mm imitation pearls
White glass beads

Shell pendant necklace:

Brandy coloured steel wire
Resin mother-of-pearl shell
Bronze seed beads and tubes
Cup tips, bead tips and spring clasp

Tools:

Wire cutters
Flat nose pliers
Scissors

Choker with white shells

Prepare 2 cords by knotting crystals into them at regular intervals. Cut 10 lengths of 'Fantasy' yarn and plait them together with the crystal strings. In the central section of the braid, stitch in the shell section pendants. Join the ends of the threads together in the bead tips and finish with a ring and bar clasp.

Difficulty level: _medium_

Designer: Maria di Spirito

Materials:

1mm cord
'Fantasy' yarn
Shell section pendants
6mm rose-cut half crystals
Small rings and pins
Bead tips and a ring and bar clasp

Tools:

Wire cutters
Round nose pliers
Scissors

Turquoise necklace with mother-of-pearl pendants

Plait together 6 waxed cords and secure them with a bead tip at either end. Alternate square shells and wooden beads of different shapes and colours and attach to the plait. Make up a variety of pendants using blue and green wooden beads that are alternated with shell chips. Finish some with mother-of-pearl pendants and attach to the necklace.

Difficulty level: complex

Designer: Maria di Spirito

Materials:

0.35mm nylon thread
1mm blue waxed cord
Mother-of-pearl pendants
Wooden beads in various shapes
and colours and square shells
Bead tips and spring clasp

Tools:

Flat nose pliers
Scissors

31

Wisteria necklace with mother-of-pearl and shell chips

To decorate the mother-of-pearl pendant, wrap the metal wire around the piece in an irregular pattern, adding a few pearls as you go along. Thread 3 strands of nylon-coated steel wire with violet shell chips, imitation pearls and 'Preciosa' bicone crystals. Pass the 3 wires through the holes of the mother-of-pearl bar and add a few more pearls. Tie the wires to the mother-of-pearl pendant.

Difficulty level: complex

Designer: Amarilli Reggiani

Materials:

Metal wire
0.45mm nylon-coated steel wire
Mother-of-pearl pendant
3mm and 6mm white imitation pearls
1 thread of shell chips
4mm 'Preciosa' bicone crystals
Bead tips
Hook fastener

Tools:

Wire cutters
Round nose pliers
Flat nose pliers

Sapphire and shell strands

Arrange groups of crystals and shells held in place by bead tips on 3 blue steel wires. Collect the 3 wires in a bead tip and fix the head of the bead tip inside a clamshell bead tip. Finish with a ring and bar clasp.

Difficulty level: easy

Designer: Maria di Spirito

Materials:

Blue nylon-coated steel wire
White, two-sided seashells
6mm and 12mm rose-cut, facetted crystals
Bead tips and 1 clamshell bead tip
Ring and bar clasp

Tools:

Cutter
Flat nose pliers

Multicoloured pearl necklace

Make up 6 steel wires with variously sized, shaped and coloured pearls. Finish each length of wire with silver spacers. Arrange 2 lengths of wire in a bead tip. Assemble 5 rings made up of small seed pearls and pass them through the hole in the mother-of-pearl pendant. Thread the necklace through.

Difficulty level: complex

Designer: Maria di Spirito

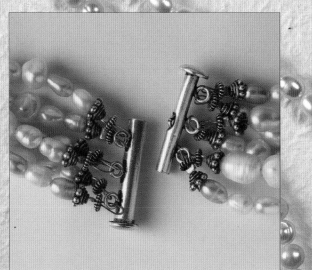

Materials:

7 threads of variously sized, shaped and coloured cultivated pearls
Silver nylon-coated steel wire
Silver spacers
Silver bayonet clasp
Bead tips
Mother-of-pearl pendant

Tools:

Wire cutters
Flat nose pliers

Bali necklace

Thread cultivated pearls and little silver spacers on 3 lengths of steel wire. Interlace the 3 wires and join them by fixing a 3-hole spacer at each of the wire ends. Continue beading using only 1 of the wires, cutting the other 2 wires. Thread silver spacers and then cultivated pearls up to the clasp. Finish with silver bead tips and a ring and bar clasp.

Difficulty level: complex

Designer: Maria di Spirito

Materials:

Silver nylon-coated steel wire
Oval and flat cultivated pearls
Silver spacers
Silver bead tips
Silver ring and bar clasp

Tools:

Wire cutters
Flat nose pliers

39

Black and white necklace

Make up 2 small circles of small black crystals and use to secure 2 mother-of-pearl pendants. Cut 25 threads of various 'Fantasy' yarns and thread the thinnest white yarns with a few little black crystals. Join the threads together and pull them through the upper pendant's crystal bead loop. Finish with bead tips and a spring clasp.

Difficulty level: medium   Designer: Maria di Spirito

Materials:

Flat and tubular 'Fantasy' yarn
4mm rosette-cut black crystals
Mother-of-pearl pendants
Clamshell tips and spring clasp

Tools:

Scissors
Flat nose pliers

'Fantasy' yarn necklace with pearls and mother-of-pearl

Put together a group of thick textured 'Fantasy' yarns and tie 4 knots in it. Attach rings made up of coloured imitation pearls in between the knots. Add a mother-of-pearl pendant attached with a ring of pearls to the centre of the necklace.

Difficulty level: medium

Designer: Maria di Spirito

Materials:

'Fantasy' yarn
0.45mm nylon-coated steel wire
Bead tips
3.6mm and 8mm imitation pearls
Mother-of-pearl pendant
Spring ring clasp

Tools:

Flat nose pliers
Scissors

Palm tree bead necklace

Cut 4 threads of 'Fantasy' yarn and decorate with palm tree beads, metal spacers and knots. Use 4 short lengths of yarn decorated with small beads and metal spacers to make a pendant. Pass through a large bead and attach to the centre of the necklace. Make the fastening with a buttonhole and a wooden bead.

Difficulty level: easy

Designer: Maria di Spirito

Materials:

Brown 'Fantasy' yarn
Palm tree beads
Metal spacers

Tools:

Scissors

Golden necklace with wooden pendants

Make up a number of pendants of various lengths by threading each pin with a variety of beads and securing each pin by twisting the wire into a little ring. Cut a number of 'Fantasy', waxed cord and organza threads. Tie regularly spaced knots into the threads, and insert the previously prepared pendants one at a time. Bring together, secure the threads in the metal tips and finish with a spring ring clasp.

Difficulty level: *medium*

Designer: Maria di Spirito

Materials:

Beads of various shapes and colours
Organza threads and 'Fantasy' waxed cord of various colours
Pins, metal wire and bead tips
Spring ring clasp

Tools:

Scissors

Strings of coloured seeds

Cut 4 nylon strands and thread each strand with alternating coloured seeds and black beads. Pass the 4 strands on each end through a large, flat bead, then continue on both sides, keeping all 4 strands together and threading with little black beads to the clasp. Tie the threads and cover the knots with clamshell bead tips. Close with a hook clasp.

Difficulty level: easy

Designer: Neria Lumiati

Materials:

Black glass beads
1 string of coloured seeds
Flat dark wood beads
Nylon thread
Clamshell bead tips
Hook clasp

Tools:

Scissors
Flat nose pliers

Seashell chips and red beads

Cut 3 lengths of nylon thread and, keeping them together, thread with alternating wooden cubes and little red beads. When you have completed approximately 12cm (4¾in), divide the threads and continue threading them separately, alternating between little red beads and seashell chips. After a few centimetres pass the 3 threads through a wooden cube and repeat. Finish the last 12cm (4¾in) with alternating wooden cubes and little red beads. Knot the threads and secure the knots in the clamshell bead tips; finish with a spring clasp. Attach the agate pendant to the centre of the necklace with the help of a short length of little red beads.

Difficulty level: medium

Designer: Neria Lumiati

Materials:

Small red glass beads
Black wooden beads
Seashell chips
Black agate pendant
Nylon thread
Clamshell bead tips
Spring clasp

Tools:

Scissors
Flat nose pliers

51

Wooden necklace with coconut pendant

Prepare 6 lengths of nylon by threading with little wooden tubes, discs and round beads. Make up 3 small circles of wooden beads and, before closing them, pass through the pendant and over the necklace. Finish the necklace with bead tips and a spring clasp.

Difficulty level: medium

Designer: Maria di Spirito

Materials:

0.35mm nylon thread
Various small wooden beads, including tubes, discs and round beads
Coconut pendant
Clamshell bead tips
Spring clasp with chain
Small rings

Tools:

Flat nose pliers
Scissors

53

Madrepore and metal spacer necklace

Alternate little rods and round beads of madrepore with metal spacers on 3 lengths of 'Fantasy' yarn. Intertwine the 3 threads, join them and secure both ends in a star-shaped spacer. Attach a group of 20 threads at the other end of each star spacer, and finish with a clamshell bead tip and a ring and bar clasp.

Difficulty level: medium

Designer: Maria di Spirito

Materials:

'Fantasy' yarn
Various metal spacers
Madrepore rods and
round beads
Shells (for the bracelet)
Clamshell bead tips
Ring and bar clasp

Tools:

Scissors
Cutter

Madrepore necklace with crystals

Make up a pendant by mounting a large madrepore bead on a pin and topping it with a metal spacer. Alternate different sizes of madrepore rods and round beads with rose-cut crystals on some steel wire. Halfway through add the madrepore pendant you prepared earlier. Finish with a hook clasp.

Difficulty level: easy

Designer: Maria di Spirito

Materials:

Gold nylon-coated steel wire
Madrepore rods and round beads
8mm and 10mm rose-cut crystals
Metal spacers
Bead pins
Hook clasp

Tools:

Wire cutters
Flat nose pliers
Scissors

Bamboo coral and silver necklace

Alternate coral heishis with small silver spacers on 3 lengths of steel wire. Intertwine the 3 threads and join them together with a 3-hole spacer at each end. Continue with just 1 of the wires, cutting off the other 2 wires. Thread with silver spacers and candy-shaped coral beads. Finish with silver spacers and a ring and bar clasp.

Difficulty level: medium

Designer: Maria di Spirito

Materials:

Red nylon-coated steel wire
Bamboo coral candy shapes and heishi
Silver spacers
Silver bead tips
Silver ring and bar clasp

Tools:

Cutter
Flat nose pliers

59

Crystal and quartz necklace

Thread the citrine quartz chips on to the nylon thread, varying the size and colour. Use the crochet hook to intertwine the thread, gradually adding the semi-precious stones as you work. Prepare 12 strings of chips with the crochet hook adding topaz crystals at the end. Divide into 2 groups of 6 strings, knot the ends and secure in the clamshell bead tips. Make several pendants by threading semi-precious stones and crystals on to pins and finishing each pin by bending the ends to form a small loop. Fasten the safety pin across all the nylon threads and insert the pendants at the centre.

Difficulty level: medium

Designer: Annarita Aloni

Materials:

0.20mm nylon thread
Various strings of citrine quartz chips
6mm and 12mm rose-cut topaz crystals
Various sizes of semi-precious stones
Safety pin and pins
Bead tips and clamshell bead tips
Hook clasp

Tools:

Wire cutters
Flat nose pliers
Crochet hook
Scissors

Choker with wooden pendant

Make 2 regularly spaced holes in the top of the pendants. Link the pendants together with some waxed string. Cut a number of threads and secure with a spiral of string, leaving 1 string to knot with the wooden pendant. Enlarge the holes on 1 side only of 2 large wooden beads and insert the strings in the enlarged holes. Close the necklace with a spring clasp and chain.

Difficulty level: *medium*

Designer: Maria di Spirito

Materials:

Wooden pendants with leaf imprint
1mm waxed string
2 large black wooden beads
Spring clasp and chain

Tools:

Scissors
Flat nose pliers

The author is an employee of Fantasy Craft of Milan, which specialises in the production and sale of jewellery supplies. It also offers courses in Venetian bead-making and beading craft.

Readers who would like to see the beads featured in the courses should visit www.fantasycraft.it

The author Maria di Spirito and her colleague Annarita Aloni photographed at Fantasy Craft